The Pirate Story

Copyright © 2023 Sarah Wallace

All rights reserved.
No part of this book may be reproduced or used in any manner without the prior written permission of the copyright owner, except for the use of brief quotations in a book review.

The Pirate Story

Manuscript: Sarah Wallace

Illustrations: VENUS ANGELICA

The Pirate Story

Author
Sarah Wallace

Illustrator
Venus Angelica

There once were seven pirates sailing the seven seas. The pirates had been looking for the island of their dreams for seven whole years.

They had heard rumors that there was a secret treasure somewhere on the island. It was a magic treasure said to hold what they love the most.

After seven long years, Pearl, a brave pirate with long red hair, suddenly spotted an island in the distance. She yelled out to her fellow pirates, "Ahoy! Look ahead! Behold the island of our dreams!"

So, they began to sail towards the island. They sang their favorite tune, "Yo-ho, yo-ho, to the island we go! Yo-ho, yo-ho, to the island we go!"

After they anchored their ship, the pirates jumped into a boat and rowed to shore. When they arrived, Pearl almost tripped over something red and shiny in the sand. She scooped it up. It was a red ruby! "What does this mean?" she whispered.

The treasure was there right under their feet! Pearl asked the other pirates to grab their shovels and dig. They sang, "Yo-ho, yo-ho, to the treasure we go! Yo-ho, yo-ho, to the treasure we go!"

A curious pirate with fabulous glasses named Jewel shouted, "I hit something hard!"

"What is it?" asked Sonny, a timid pirate with bright blonde hair like the sun. It was a large treasure chest! So Pearl, Jewel, Sonny, and all the other pirates grabbed onto the treasure chest and started to pull. "Heave-ho, heave ho!"

Slowly, they pulled the heavy chest out of the sand. The pirates were so happy to have found the special treasure. But Pearl noticed something. She said, "Pirates, there is a lock but no key! What should we do?"

Jewel noticed a clue carved on a stone beside the lock. It read, 'If you find where the bunny lives, you will find the key that fits the lock.' The seven pirates set out on a search for the key.

They sang, "Yo-ho, yo-ho, to the key we go! Yo-ho, yo-ho, to the key we go!"

There was a forest at the edge of the beach. As the pirates entered the forest, a fox approached them. Sonny asked the fox, "Fox, do you know where the bunny lives?"

The fox licked his lips and said, "I don't know, but if you do find that bunny, be sure to let me know." Sonny was scared of the fox so he asked the others to run away as fast as they could.

Oh no! Pearl tripped on a hole in the ground. She called, "Wait! It looks like this could be where the bunny lives."

Jewel reached her hand in the hole and said, "I feel something soft. What do you think it is?"

"It must be the bunny!" Jewel said. Then the bunny jumped out and hopped away. Jewel kept reaching around and felt something hard. "What is that?" she asked. She pulled out a golden key. "I found it!" she exclaimed. The pirates were so excited they jumped up and down.

A strong pirate named Scully said, "We better run back to the treasure to see if this key fits the lock!" The seven pirates ran as quickly as they could. This time, they sang even faster. "Yo-ho, yo-ho to the treasure we go! Yo-ho, yo-ho to the treasure we go!"

But when the pirates arrived at the beach, the treasure chest was gone! Jewel cried out, "Now we will never find what we love the most!" Then, she pointed at the wet sand, exclaiming, "Look at the paw prints! They are so big! Could they be bear prints, Pearl?"

Pearl said, "Well, we should follow these paw prints. Maybe a bear stole our treasure!" The pirates followed the tracks up a grassy hill. They passed a big blueberry patch and stopped to pick a bunch for their walk.

The tracks led to a deep, dark cave. Pearl approached the cave and yelled, "Hello, is there anyone there?"

They heard a loud voice that said, "Who dares bother me while I sleep!" A very large bear crawled out of the cave.

Pearl stood her ground. She said confidently, "We think you have our treasure. That is ours. We had it first and found it fair and square."

The bear growled, "Well too bad. It's all mine now!"

The pirates looked at each other. Sonny said softly, "What do we do?"

Then Pearl remembered her basket of delicious blueberries. "Bear, could we trade?" asked Pearl.

The bear said, "Well isn't that nice, I will need those for my long winter nap." So, they traded the treasure for the berries. After all, the bear did not know about the magic inside the treasure chest, or else he might have never considered the trade.

The pirates lugged their treasure to a safe place on the beach. Jewel was so excited to see the treasure that held all the things they loved the most. She took the golden key and unlocked the chest.

Inside, Jewel saw her favorite stuffed animal that she had lost over seven years ago. Pearl saw that there was so much candy, she thought she would have to share it with the other pirates so she wouldn't eat it all. And Sonny saw a little puppy he had always wanted.

Each of the seven pirates looked inside the treasure chest and discovered what they wished for most. They were all smiling from ear to ear. Just then, Jewel noticed something shiny at the bottom of the chest. "Look! What is that?" she asked.

All the pirates saw their own faces reflected back at them. "Is that a mirror?" Jewel asked.

It turns out, it was a mirror. The pirates realized something truly important: this treasure held what they loved the most, and what they **really** loved the most was themselves and each other.

www.ingramcontent.com/pod-product-compliance
Lightning Source LLC
Chambersburg PA
CBHW041541040426
42446CB00002B/185